TIME MANAGEMENT AND PRODUCTIVITY

MASTERING YOUR TIME FOR MAXIMUM EFFICIENCY

INTRODUCTION

Here, in *"Time Management and Productivity: Mastering Your Time for Maximum Efficiency,"* we'll take a revolutionary step toward taking back control of our most valuable resource: time. Time management and productivity enhancement are more important than ever in this fast-paced world when demands compete for our attention all the time and distractions are everywhere.

This booklet is more than just a compilation of time-saving strategies for jam-packing our already full schedules with tasks. Rather, it is a thorough investigation of the complex interplay among production, time, and individual efficacy. As we go deeper into this topic, we will unearth significant ideas, doable tactics, and useful tools that will enable you to make the most of your time and increase your productivity in all spheres of your life.

Our investigation is based on the knowledge that time is a valuable resource that should be used carefully rather than just as a resource to be used. We will explore the psychology of time management, looking at our attitudes, convictions, and routines related to time, and identifying the ingrained patterns that might be impeding our capacity to maximize our time.

The idea of prioritization—the skill of determining what really matters and focusing our attention and energy on those priorities—is fundamental to our path. We'll go over a variety of prioritization strategies, such as the traditional Eisenhower matrix and the more sophisticated ways of value-based prioritization, so you may decide where to focus your time and energy.

We shall face the ubiquitous problems of procrastination and distraction as we negotiate the intricacies of contemporary living. We will identify the root reasons of these productivity traps and provide you with doable solutions, such as developing focus and mindfulness or putting in place efficient boundary-setting tactics.

However, efficient time management and productivity go beyond simply finishing tasks; they also include pursuing meaningful objectives and aspirations, cultivating balance and well-being, and integrating work and life in a holistic manner. We will discuss methods for taking care of your physical and emotional well-being, striking a healthy work-life balance, and coordinating your activities with your priorities and values.

This ebook contains a plethora of knowledge gained from the disciplines of organizational behavior, psychology, and neuroscience. It also includes activities and examples from everyday life to help you put the knowledge to use in your own life. This ebook is your comprehensive guide to mastering time management for maximum efficiency, whether you're a busy professional trying to balance multiple responsibilities, an aspiring entrepreneur looking to maximize your productivity, or just an individual looking to reclaim control of your time and life.

I encourage you to approach the material with an open mind and a readiness to question your pre-existing habits and beliefs as we set out on this adventure together. The path to mastery is not always simple, but with commitment, perseverance, and the appropriate techniques, you can maximize your time and make significant, positive changes in your life. So let's set out on this adventure together, regaining control over our time and building a fulfilling, productive, and purposeful existence.

Chapter 2

UNDERSTANDING TIME MANAGEMENT

*T*ime management is more than just a catchphrase or a collection of methods for planning your calendar. It is a basic ability that enables people to maximize their time constraints and accomplish their objectives effectively and efficiently. The fundamental purpose of time management is to deliberately allot time to tasks and activities in accordance with their significance and priority, with the ultimate objective being to maximize output and reduce wasteful time.

Importance of Effective Time Management

Reaching Goals: People who have good time management skills are able to set priorities for their duties and devote time to things that help them reach their goals. People can move closer to their goals in a methodical and effective way by practicing time management.

Enhanced Productivity: People who are adept in time management are able to utilize their time to the fullest, which boosts production and productivity. One can do more in less time by concentrating on high-priority projects and minimizing time spent on low-value activities.

Decreased Stress: People who struggle to meet deadlines and balance conflicting expectations frequently experience emotions of overload and stress as a result of poor time management. People can feel less stressed and have more mental serenity by using efficient time management techniques.

Higher-Quality Work: People can generate work that meets or above expectations if they give projects enough time and avoid rushing deadlines. Superior results can be achieved by careful job preparation, execution, and review, all made possible by efficient time management.

Improved Work-Life Balance: People who are good at managing their time can set aside time for hobbies, relationships, and personal pursuits in addition to work-related obligations. People can feel happier and more fulfilled overall by finding a balance between their personal and professional lives.

To put it simply, effective time management is a fundamental ability that supports success in all facets of life. People can reach their goals, realize their full potential, and enjoy happy, productive lives by becoming proficient in time management.

Time Management Psychology: Understanding Your Relationship with Time

Every person has a varied perception and experience of time, which is a distinct and limited resource. A complex interaction of psychological, societal, and environmental elements shapes our relationship with time, affecting how we value, interpret, and use it. To create efficient time management plans and get over typical roadblocks, it's vital to comprehend the psychology of time management.

Time Perception: The subjective sense of time passing that varies greatly amongst individuals is referred to as time perception.

Age, personality, and cultural background are a few examples of factors that might affect how people view time. For instance, some people could naturally be more timely and time-conscious than others, who might take a more laid-back and adaptable approach to time management.

Views and Attitudes about Time:

How we prioritize and manage our time is shaped by our attitudes and beliefs about time. While negative attitudes toward time, such as perfectionism or procrastination, might impede productivity, positive attitudes toward time, like appreciating efficiency and timeliness, can help with successful time management.

Our time management practices are also significantly influenced by our beliefs about the availability or scarcity of time. People who feel as though they don't have enough time may feel under pressure to fit as many activities as they can into their calendars, which can result in stress and burnout. On the other hand, people who believe that time is abundant might handle time management in a more carefree and adaptable manner.

Time Personality Traits: Stable individual variations in how people approach and manage their time are referred to as time personality traits. Numerous time personality qualities, including time urgency, time orientation, and time perspective, have been found through research to have an impact on time management practices.

People with high time urgency, for instance, could always feel under pressure to finish things fast and effectively, whereas people with low time urgency might go more slowly.

Time Management Styles: These are the methods and approaches people employ to plan, organize, and prioritize their time. Depending on their specific tastes, objectives, and situations, various people may use different time management techniques.

Approaches that are linear, adaptable, and structured are common time management styles. While flexible thinkers tend to modify their schedules in response to changing situations, linear thinkers prefer to arrange their time in a sequential and logical manner. Regular schedules and routines are what structured thinkers thrive on, and they want to arrange their time in advance. The first step to developing better time management abilities is realizing how you relate to time. You can pinpoint opportunities for development and create individualized time-management techniques by gaining awareness of your time attitudes, beliefs, personality traits, and management styles.

Typical Time Management Difficulties and Obstacles

Even with the best of intentions, a lot of us have trouble managing our time because we fall victim to frequent mistakes and difficulties that reduce our effectiveness and productivity. Understanding these traps is crucial to creating workable solutions that help us avoid them and advance our time management abilities.

Procrastination: Procrastination is the propensity to put off or postpone responsibilities, frequently as a result of unease, uneasiness, or a lack of desire. Missed deadlines, elevated stress levels, and decreased productivity can result from procrastinating.

Perfectionism, fear of failing, and a lack of direction or clarity are common reasons for procrastinating. Additionally, procrastination may be a sign of deeper problems like low self-worth or ineffective time management techniques.

Ineffective Planning and Organization: Ineffective planning and organization can result in confusion, inefficiency, and time loss. In the absence of a well-defined strategy or framework, tasks can be disregarded, deadlines missed, and priorities ignored.

A persistent feeling of overwhelm, disorganized workplaces, and missed appointments are all signs of poor planning and organization. Even the best-intentioned attempts at time management may fall short in the absence of a strong planning and organizing base.

Overcommitment and Overload: When people take on more obligations or tasks than they can reasonably do, they become overly committed, which can result in feelings of exhaustion and burnout. The term "overload" describes a condition of extreme bustle or mental congestion in which people find it difficult to concentrate and set priorities.

Overload and overcommitment can result from a number of things, including difficulties saying no, fear of missing out (FOMO), and unreasonable expectations. Without limits and boundaries, people could always be chasing deadlines and finding it difficult to fulfill their responsibilities.

Distractions and Interruptions: With emails, social media updates, and continuous notifications competing for our attention, distractions and interruptions are a common occurrence in the modern digital world. Distractions have the power to break our concentration, interfere with our job, cause time wastage, and lower our productivity.

Distractions from social media, cellphones, multitasking, and background noise are commonplace. People could struggle to finish projects quickly and successfully if they don't have any techniques in place to reduce distractions and stay focused.

Individuals can improve their productivity and effectiveness by developing ways to improve their time management abilities by recognizing and addressing these typical mistakes and problems. We will examine useful methods and resources for resolving these issues and managing our time effectively in the ensuing chapters.

Chapter 2

ASSESSING YOUR TIME

***P**erforming a Time Audit: Gaining an understanding of your current time usage*

Understanding how we now distribute our time resources is necessary before we can manage our time effectively. One effective method for understanding our time usage habits and pinpointing opportunities for development is to do a time audit.

Establish Your Time Audit Methodology: To start, decide how long your audit will take, such as a week, two weeks, or month. Choose a method for keeping track of your time: a journal, a spreadsheet, or a digital application. When you log your activities, be sure to be precise and consistent.

Take Note of Your Actions: Keep a careful journal of your daily activities for the whole allotted period. Be specific and detailed in your notes, including personal activities, leisure time, and any unplanned disruptions or diversions in addition to work-related responsibilities.

Examine Your Results: After finishing your time audit, check over the activities you recorded and group them into general categories (such work, play, and personal errands). Determine the patterns and trends in the way you use your time—where do you spend most of it? Which activities take up more time than they should on a regular basis?

Examine Your Priorities: Examine how you use your time in relation to your priorities and objectives. Are you spending enough time on things that support your goals and values? Is there any place where you could reorganize your time to better assist your objectives?

Find Improvement Opportunities: Make use of the knowledge you acquired from your time audit to find areas that could use improvement. Are there any tasks that can be assigned or made more efficient? Are there any distractions or time wasters that you can cut down on or get rid of?

Iterate and Adjust: Time audits are a continuous process of self-awareness and development rather than a one-time event. Perform time audits on a regular basis to monitor your development, spot shifts in your time-use habits, and make any corrections.

You can find areas for improvement and obtain important insights into how you currently spend your time by carrying out a complete time audit. Equipped with this understanding, you may proactively manage your time such that it complements your objectives and priorities.

Recognizing Distractions and Time Wasters

Recognizing time wasters and diversions is crucial to regaining control over our time and increasing productivity in today's world of continual interruptions and distractions.

Identify typical Time Wasters: To begin, determine which typical time wasters are consuming your time and energy. These can include multitasking, procrastination, pointless meetings, spending too much time on social media, and ineffective workflows or procedures.

Monitor Your Diversions: Keep an eye out for the particular distractions that cause you to lose focus and become less productive. Are those notifications and incoming emails? Unexpected calls or visits from relatives or coworkers? internal diversions like daydreaming or straying thoughts?

Evaluate the Effect on Your Level of Production: Consider the effects these diversions and time wasters have on your effectiveness and production. Do they result in a feeling of overload, more stress, or missed deadlines? Recognizing the negative effects of these distractions can inspire action to reduce them.

Put Strategies to Reduce Distractions into Practice: After you've determined which of your main sources of distractions and time wasters are distracting you, create plans to reduce or eliminate them. This may be establishing limits on your availability and time, disabling notifications while working intently, or using strategies and tools to increase focus and attention.

Establish a Space Free from Distractions: Establish a specific area for work that is distraction-free and productive. Reduce clutter, improve lighting and ergonomics, and eliminate any possible sources of interruption to establish a workspace that encourages concentrated concentration.

Practice Mindfulness and Presence: To lessen the influence of distractions and improve your capacity to remain attentive and involved in your daily activities, cultivate mindfulness and presence. You may improve your productivity and develop your attention span by using methods like single-tasking, deep breathing exercises, and mindfulness meditation.

You may make your environment more productive and focused by recognizing and eliminating time wasters and distractions. This will help you maximize your time and work toward your objectives more quickly.

Organizing Your Goals and Priorities for Efficient Time Management

Setting clear priorities and objectives is the first step towards efficient time management. You may make sure that you move closer to your most essential goals by focusing your time and attention on the things that really matter by establishing clear objectives and priorities.

Think About Your Goals and Values: To start, consider your long-term goals, aspirations, and values. Which aspects of your life—career, relationships, health, and personal development—are the most crucial? In each of these categories, what objectives do you hope to accomplish?

Determine What Your High-Impact Tasks Are: Ascertain which of your activities are most important to achieving your priorities and goals. Your top priority are these high-impact tasks, and you should devote most of your time and energy to them.

Apply the 80/20 Rule: To prioritize your tasks and activities, use the Pareto Principle, sometimes referred to as the 80/20 rule. Determine which 20% of the activities produce 80% of the results, and then allocate your attention to these high-impact tasks first.

Establish SMART objectives: Make sure your objectives are time-bound, relevant, quantifiable, achievable, and specific (SMART). Make sure you have a clear understanding of your goals, how you plan to measure progress, and when. To make highly ambitious objectives more achievable, break them down into smaller, more doable steps.

Establish a Priority Action Plan: Create a prioritized action plan that lists the things you must do in order to accomplish your objectives. Sort the tasks in order of importance and urgency, then allot your time to the most important and urgent ones.

Regularly Evaluate and Modify Your Priorities: As situations change and new opportunities present themselves, goals and priorities may also. Make any necessary revisions to your priorities and goals after reviewing them frequently to make sure they are in line with your values and aspirations.

You may concentrate your time and energy on tasks that get you closer to your goals and cut down on distractions and time wasters by clearly defining your priorities and goals. You can maximize your time and accomplish your objectives effectively and efficiently if you have a strong sense of purpose and direction.

Chapter 3

STRATEGIES FOR EFFECTIVE TIME MANAGEMENT

We need to empower ourselves with a repertoire of efficient time management techniques in order to maximize our efficiency in managing our time. These tactics, which range from task management programs to goal-setting and prioritization methods, give us the structure and direction we need to maximize our time and accomplish our goals in a clear and purposeful manner.

Prioritization Methods: ABC Prioritization, Eisenhower Matrix, etc.

The key to efficient time management is setting priorities, which helps us concentrate our time and effort on the projects and activities that will have the biggest effects. We can decide where to concentrate our resources and make sure we are focusing on what is really important by using prioritization approaches like the Eisenhower Matrix and ABC prioritization.

Eisenhower Matrix: Also referred to as the Urgent-Important Matrix, this matrix is a useful tool for setting priorities for projects according to their significance and urgency. It divides tasks into four sections:
Quadrant 1: Urgent and Important (Do First): This category includes tasks that are essential to reaching your objectives and call for quick attention.
Tasks that can be scheduled and completed later but are crucial for long-term success are in Quadrant 2: Important but Not Urgent (Schedule).
Quadrant 3: Urgent but Not Important (Delegate) - Can be assigned to others are tasks that are urgent but don't make a big difference in achieving your objectives.
Tasks that fall into the fourth quadrant, "Not Urgent and Not Important (Eliminate)," can be reduced or deleted because they are neither urgent nor significant.
You can focus your attention on high-impact activities that are in line with your beliefs and goals by methodically classifying tasks into these quadrants.
ABC prioritizing: ABC prioritizing is a straightforward but efficient method for allocating tasks according to their urgency and significance. A, B, or C are the letters given to tasks according on their priority level:
A Task: Critical and urgent tasks with a high priority. These are the things that should come first since they need to be done right now.
B Tasks: Important but not urgent, medium-priority tasks. These assignments ought to be finished after the A jobs.
C chores: Non-urgent, low-importance chores with a low priority. If at all possible, these responsibilities can be assigned or postponed.
You may make sure that you are devoting your time and effort to projects that advance your long-term goals and objectives by prioritizing them using the ABC technique.
Other Prioritization Strategies: To efficiently manage your time, you can employ a number of different prioritization strategies in addition to the Eisenhower Matrix and ABC prioritization. These include the Pareto Principle (concentrating on the 20% of tasks that give 80% of the outcomes), the Ivy Lee technique (prioritizing and focusing on six critical tasks each day), and the 1-3-5 rule (deciding which one big task, three medium tasks, and five little chores to handle each day).
You may make wise judgments about where to spend your time and energy by using prioritizing techniques in your time management arsenal. This will help you focus on tasks and activities that are in line with your priorities and goals.

Creating Action Plans and SMART Goals

Effective time management requires setting specific, attainable goals that serve as a road map for your desired destination and your intended course of action. By adhering to the SMART criteria, which stands for specified, measurable, attainable, relevant, and time-bound, you can make sure that your objectives are clear and feasible, hence increasing your chances of success.

Detailed: There should be no room for doubt or ambiguity in the goals, which should be well-defined and detailed. Give a clear explanation of your goals, their significance, and the actions necessary to reach them.

As an illustration, instead of aiming for something general like "increase productivity," try something more targeted like "increase daily sales by 10% within the next quarter."

Measurable objectives enable you to monitor your progress and assess your level of achievement. Establish precise measurements or standards for tracking your progress and decide how you'll know when the objective has been attained.

For instance, instead of aiming to "get in shape," make your objective attainable by putting it in the form of "lose 10 pounds in the next three months."

Achievable: Considering your existing resources, abilities, and limitations, your goals should be reasonable and doable. Establish objectives that will challenge you yet are doable with hard work and dedication.

An example of a more realistic goal would be to "complete a beginner Spanish course and hold a basic conversation within three months," as opposed to an overly ambitious one like "become fluent in Spanish in three months."

Relevant: Your goals ought to be pertinent and in line with your priorities, values, and long-term goals. Make sure the objective fits with your overarching success vision and has significance.

Example: Choose a goal that is in line with your hobbies and aspirations rather than one that is unconnected to your work or personal goals, such as "complete a professional certification in my field within the next year."

Time-Bound: Objectives ought to have a precisely defined completion date or schedule. Establish clear deadlines or benchmarks for the goal's completion to instill a sense of urgency and responsibility.

For instance, make a time-bound objective like "finish the first draft of my book within six months" as opposed to an open-ended one like "write a book someday."

You may make your intentions clear, concentrate your efforts, and improve your chances of success by creating SMART goals. Creating action plans that list the procedures needed to accomplish each goal can also act as a roadmap for implementation, directing your efforts and guaranteeing that you don't get off course.

Developing Task Management Programs and To-Do Lists That Work

Every efficient time manager's toolkit must include to-do lists since they offer a concrete list of things that need to get done. You can stay focused, productive, and organized while making sure that nothing gets missed by using task management tools and making efficient to-do lists.

Organize Your To-Do Lists: Start by arranging your lists of tasks in a style that suits you best. Regardless of your preference for digital or analog formats, go with an intuitive and user-friendly solution. Sort your to-do lists into parts or categories according to the project, priority, or context.

Set Task Priorities:

Sort the things on your lists of things to accomplish according to their priority and urgency. Sort activities according to importance and decide which ones need to be completed right away by using the prioritization strategies we covered before, such as ABC prioritization or the Eisenhower Matrix.

Divide Up the Tasks:
Divide more complex jobs into smaller, easier-to-manage subtasks. This gives tasks a clearer path for execution and also increases their doable level. When describing a task, use action verbs to incorporate certain information or specifications.

Establish deadlines:
Give each item on your to-do lists a deadline or due date. This instills a sense of accountability and urgency that spurs you to act and finish activities on time. When establishing deadlines, be reasonable and consider how long each work will take to do.

Examine and Update Frequently:
Make sure your to-do lists are up to date and pertinent by reviewing and updating them on a regular basis. As new tasks come up, add them, delete completed ones, and reorder the order of importance as necessary. Make effective use of your to-do lists as a flexible tool to help you manage your time and fulfill your obligations.

Put Task Management Systems into Practice:
To improve efficiency and optimize your workflow, think about putting task management systems or technologies into place. You have many options to help you efficiently plan and manage your work, ranging from basic to-do list apps to complex project management tools. You can stay productive, focused, and organized by making good to-do lists and putting task management systems in place. This will help you make the most of your time and reach your goals with clarity and purpose.

By adding these techniques to your time management toolkit, you will be able to focus on tasks and activities that are in line with your priorities and goals and make well-informed decisions about where to spend your time and energy. By establishing well-defined priorities, attainable objectives, and efficient task management frameworks, you can optimize your productivity and accomplish your goals with assurance and determination.

Chapter 4

BOOSTING PRODUCTIVITY

Increasing productivity is critical to our efforts to optimize efficiency and become experts in time management. Being productive is working smarter, making the most use of our resources, and accomplishing more with less effort rather than just working harder or longer hours. This chapter explores a number of methods and approaches to increase productivity, such as overcoming procrastination, controlling energy, and making good use of technology.

Strategies for Increasing Motivation and Overcoming Procrastination

The enemy of productivity, procrastination saps our motivation and prevents us from achieving our objectives. A mix of self-awareness, self-discipline, and efficient time and task management techniques is needed to overcome procrastination. The following strategies will help you become more motivated and overcome procrastination:

Divide Up the Work into Doable Steps: Due to their overwhelming nature, big or difficult activities might cause people to put them off. To make jobs less daunting and easier to complete, break them down into smaller, more manageable chunks. One tiny step at a time is what you should concentrate on finishing, gaining momentum and drive along the way.

Define your objectives and deadlines:
Set precise due dates for tasks and clearly outline your objectives. A well-defined direction and aim can boost motivation and lower the probability of putting things off. Make sure your goals are time-bound, relevant, measurable, and specific by using the SMART criterion.

Apply the Pomodoro Method:
A time-management technique called the Pomodoro Technique divides work into periods, usually lasting 25 minutes, and then takes brief breaks in between. Set a timer for the amount of time you want to spend working, concentrate on the task at hand, and take a quick break when the timer goes off. This method, which offers set work intervals and regular breaks, can improve focus and productivity.

Develop Self-Compassion: Fear of failing, perfectionism, or self-defeating thoughts are common causes of procrastination. By accepting and embracing your flaws, forgiving yourself for your errors, and changing your negative ideas to positive ones, you can cultivate self-compassion. It can be simpler to overcome procrastination when self-compassion is developed because it can boost resilience and motivation.

Establish a Productive Environment: Concentration and motivation are greatly influenced by your surroundings. Establish a dedicated workspace that is noise-, clutter-, and distraction-free. Make sure you are surrounded by cues that inspire you, such as motivating sayings, pictures, or items that represent your ambitions.

Give Yourself a Treat:
Give yourself a reward when you accomplish goals and milestones. Honor your progress toward your objectives and celebrate your successes, no matter how minor. Rewarding oneself with a favorite food, a leisure activity, or a break can be as easy as that.

Through the application of these strategies for conquering procrastination and boosting motivation, you may develop a goal-oriented mentality and take proactive measures with determination, clarity, and focus.

Techniques for Controlling Energy and Preventing Burnout

Maintaining long-term productivity and preventing burnout need effective energy management. Energy is a renewable resource that can be refilled by wise lifestyle decisions and self-care routines, in contrast to time, which is limited and fixed. The following are some methods for controlling energy levels and avoiding burnout:

Make Self-Care a Priority: Maintaining one's physical, mental, and emotional well-being requires self-care. Make time for things that will help you feel better physically and mentally, like exercise, a balanced diet, enough sleep, mindfulness exercises, and relaxation techniques. To make sure you are taking care of yourself completely, make time in your daily schedule for self-care activities.

Work-Life Integration: This is the process of combining work and personal life in a way that enhances wellbeing, fulfillment, and balance. Rather than aiming for a rigid division of your personal and professional lives, discover methods to combine obligations and activities in a way that promotes your general well-being. Establish limits on work hours, give leisure time top priority, and schedule time for relationships, hobbies, and self-care.

Effectively Handle Stress: Although stress is a normal part of life, prolonged or severe stress can cause burnout and lower productivity. Reduce tension and increase relaxation by using stress-reduction strategies such progressive muscle relaxation, deep breathing, meditation, and visualization. Determine the stressors in your life and create coping mechanisms to deal with them.

Take Regular Breaks: Staying focused, productive, and creative requires regular breaks. Plan regular downtime throughout the day to allow your body and mind to recuperate from moments of high activity or concentration. During breaks, take part in rejuvenating and calming activities like taking a stroll, meditating, or interacting with coworkers.

Set Limits:

To avoid overload and overcommitment, set clear boundaries for your time, energy, and attention. When an obligation or request conflicts with your priorities or principles, learn to say no. Establish reasonable expectations for both yourself and other people, and politely and assertively express your boundaries.

Keep an eye on your energy levels:

Throughout the day, keep an eye on your energy levels and modify your schedule as necessary. Determine the times of day that you are most awake and productive, then arrange your busiest work for these times. When you're feeling down, take a break or move on to something easier to keep yourself from burning out and continue working productively.

You may maintain high levels of productivity and well-being over time by putting these techniques for controlling energy levels and preventing burnout into practice. This will guarantee that you can accomplish your objectives and prosper in all facets of your life.

Using Tools and Technology to Increase Productivity

The digital era of today provides a wealth of tools and resources that can be used to improve productivity and better manage time. Using technology to automate repetitive chores, enhance cooperation and communication, and streamline workflows is possible with apps for task management and time-tracking. The following are some strategies for increasing productivity with technology and tools:

Task Management Apps: Digital platforms for prioritizing, monitoring, and organizing activities and projects are offered by task management apps like Asana, Trello, and Todoist. With the help of these applications, you can make to-do lists, assign tasks to team members, establish deadlines, and track advancement in real time. For optimal productivity, pick a task management tool that fits your tastes and process, then incorporate it into your daily schedule.

Software for Tracking Time:

With time-tracking apps like Harvest, RescueTime, and Toggl, you can keep an eye on your time usage and pinpoint areas that need work. These programs track the amount of time spent on various projects and activities, produce in-depth reports and analytics, and provide you insight into your work patterns. To find time wasters, streamline your processes, and make data-driven decisions about how best to spend your time, use time-tracking software.

Calendar apps: You can manage your schedule, appointments, and deadlines more effectively by using calendar apps like Apple Calendar, Google Calendar, and Microsoft Outlook. With the help of these apps, you can plan meetings, create reminders, and synchronize your calendar across several devices for easy collaboration and access. Make advantage of calendar software to arrange meetings and appointments, set out time for concentrated work, and keep your schedule controlled and orderly.

Note-Taking applications: Digital platforms for gathering, arranging, and storing information are offered by note-taking applications like Evernote, OneNote, and Notion. With the use of these tools, you may take notes, make lists of things to accomplish, brainstorm, and work together in a centralized and easily accessible manner. To keep yourself organized and productive, use note-taking tools to write down crucial information and arrange your thoughts.

Platforms for Communication and Collaboration: Real-time communication, teamwork, and collaboration are made easier by platforms for communication and collaboration like Slack, Microsoft Teams, and Zoom. These platforms allow you to work together on projects regardless of location, hold virtual meetings, share files and documents, and interact with coworkers. To improve productivity in remote or distributed teams, encourage cooperation, and expedite communication, make use of communication and collaboration technologies.

Automation technologies: You may automate tedious operations and optimize workflows with automation technologies like Zapier, IFTTT, and Microsoft Power Automate. Using these tools, you may develop automated actions, triggers, and workflows that reduce manual labor and boost productivity. To save time and effort on repetitive chores, integrate various apps and services, and automate routine procedures, use automation technologies.

You may optimize your time and resources for optimal efficiency, automate repetitive processes, and streamline workflows by utilizing technology and tools to increase productivity. To reach your objectives more quickly and easily, try out a variety of tools and methods until you find the ones that work best for you. Then, implement those strategies and tools into your daily routine.

Chapter 5

TIME BLOCKING AND SCHEDULING

***T**he* key to efficient time management is the capacity to assign time to tasks and activities that are in line with our priorities and goals. With the help of effective time management strategies like time blocking and scheduling, we can organize our days to increase output, reduce distractions, and promote attention. This chapter covers the fundamentals of time blocking, its advantages, methods for making daily and weekly calendars, and ways to keep scheduling flexible and adaptive.

Overview of Time Blocking: Benefits and Principles

As a time management strategy, time blocking entails breaking up your day into discrete time blocks and assigning particular tasks or activities to each block. You may enhance your productivity, provide structure and clarity in your calendar, and sustain attention and momentum throughout the day by allocating specific time for certain work categories. The following are some time blocking guidelines and advantages:

Clarity and Focus: By outlining exactly how you will spend your time each day, time blocking helps you to stay focused and clear. You may remove uncertainty and decision fatigue by setting up certain blocks of time for various jobs or activities. This will free up your time to concentrate on the current activity without interruptions.

Planning and Prioritization: You may plan your time and assign activities based on their urgency and importance by using time blocking. You may make sure that you are giving the things that help you achieve your goals and objectives enough time and attention by making a schedule in advance and setting aside time for high-priority chores.

Enhanced Productivity: By giving your calendar structure and accountability, time blocking increases productivity. Setting aside certain time slots for various tasks fosters a sense of urgency and momentum that propels forward motion. Additionally, time blocking reduces the possibility of putting off tasks and wasting time on unimportant ones.

Decreased Multitasking and Distractions: By promoting single-tasking and concentrated work periods, time blocking reduces distractions and discourages multitasking. You can increase your focus and efficiency by committing unbroken blocks of time to particular projects, which lessens the urge to flip between them or give in to distractions.

Improved Work-Life Balance: Time blocking enables you to set aside time for personal pursuits, hobbies, and self-care in addition to work-related responsibilities. You can take care of every part of your well-being and prevent burnout by finding a balance between your personal and professional lives.

Adaptability and Flexibility: Although time blocking offers direction and structure, it also permits you to be flexible and adaptable with your scheduling. Your time blocks can be changed as necessary to take into account shifting priorities, unforeseen circumstances, or events, keeping you flexible and adaptable to the demands of everyday life.

All things considered, time blocking is an incredibly successful method for improving productivity, controlling your schedule better, and feeling more fulfilled and in charge of your everyday activities.

Planning Your Week and Day to Be as Effective as Possible

A crucial element of efficient time management is making daily and weekly schedules, which serve as a guide for allocating your time and resources in order to accomplish your goals. The following techniques can be used to create a daily and weekly timetable that will maximize efficiency:

Begin by determining your priorities:
Establish your priorities and daily or weekly objectives first. Which chores or activities are the most crucial for you to complete? Which obligations or deadlines do you need to prioritize? When organizing your calendar, refer to your priorities.

Set Aside Time for Important Tasks:

Set up certain time slots for important projects or high-priority chores that need concentration and concentrated attention. Plan these chores for the morning or early afternoon, when you are most aware and productive of the day.

Maintain a Balance in Your Schedule:

By allotting time for various chores and activities, including work, personal, and leisure pursuits, you may maintain a balanced schedule. Don't pack too many activities or responsibilities into your schedule; instead, leave time for pauses and relaxation so that you can refuel.

Be adaptable and realistic:

Be realistic about the amount of work you can complete in the allotted time, and provide room in your calendar for flexibility and adaptation. Give yourself extra time between jobs and appointments to accommodate unforeseen cancellations or delays, and be ready to modify your plans as necessary.

Employ Time Blocking Strategies:

To organize your schedule into discrete time slots for various jobs and activities, use time blocking approaches. To optimize efficiency and productivity, set out time for particular chores, appointments, meetings, and breaks. Then, follow your plan as precisely as possible.

Regularly review and make adjustments:

To make sure that your calendar stays in line with your aims and objectives, review and tweak it frequently. Consider what went well and what may be done better at the conclusion of each day or week, and change your schedule as necessary to maximize efficiency.

You may enhance productivity, reduce distractions, and find more balance and fulfillment in your everyday activities by making a weekly and daily plan that matches your priorities, goals, and values.

Scheduling Flexibility and Adaptability: Handling Unexpected Changes

Even with our best efforts, life will inevitably bring forth unforeseen changes and disturbances to our planned and organized schedules. The capacity to be flexible and adaptable is crucial for handling unforeseen changes and continuing to be productive when faced with uncertainty. The following techniques can help you handle unforeseen changes to your schedule:

Embrace a Growth mentality: Develop a growth mentality by seeing obstacles and failures as chances for improvement. Seek chances for adaptation and creativity instead of becoming overwhelmed by unforeseen events or opposing change. Instead, approach them with curiosity and resilience.

Remain Calm and collected: Remain collected and calm in the face of unforeseen changes or disruptions; try not to react hastily or angrily. Inhale deeply, evaluate the circumstances calmly, and create a plan of action grounded in knowledge and facts rather than anxiety or panic.

Task Prioritization and Resource Reallocation: Set priorities for tasks and activities according to their significance and urgency. As demands and priorities change, adjust resources accordingly. Be ready to rearrange your time blocks and reorder your priorities to make room for unforeseen obligations or chores.

Keep Lines of Communication Open: When your availability or schedule changes, keep lines of communication open with stakeholders, clients, and coworkers. Notify them of any changes or delays, and work with them to resolve any issues or problems that come up in a way that is acceptable to both of you.

Utilize time management strategies:
Rely on time management strategies like delegation, prioritization, and time blocking to keep your concentration and productivity even in the face of unforeseen events. To prevent feeling overwhelmed, divide jobs into smaller, more manageable steps and concentrate on finishing one activity at a time.

Take Advice from Experience
Make the most of unforeseen adjustments and disruptions as chances for introspection and education. After resolving a difficult circumstance or adjusting to a new routine, consider what went well and what could be improved. Then, apply those learnings to new circumstances.

You can handle unforeseen changes with resilience and confidence if you practice flexibility and adaptability in your scheduling, which will keep you productive and focused on your priorities and goals.

Chapter 6

MANAGING DISTRACTIONS AND INTERRUPTIONS

In today's age of perpetual connectedness and information overload, the ability to control interruptions and distractions has become essential to preserving focus and productivity. Email notifications, social media alerts, and unforeseen interruptions from coworkers or family members are just a few examples of the various ways that distractions can occur. It takes awareness, self-control, and the application of tactics and procedures to reduce distractions' negative effects on our time and attention. This chapter covers a number of topics, including the definition and relevance of time management, common interruptions and diversions, methods for reducing distractions and maintaining attention, and the value of setting boundaries and establishing a positive work environment.

Outlining Time Management Concepts and Their Importance

Planning, arranging, and setting priorities for tasks and activities in order to maximize available time is the process of time management. It entails setting priorities and goals, allocating time and resources appropriately, and putting plans into action to reduce downtime and increase productivity. Effective time management is crucial for accomplishing both personal and professional objectives, preserving equilibrium and overall health, and meeting obligations and duties. People who are proficient in time management can increase their output, lower their stress levels, and feel more in control and satisfied with their lives.

Recognizing Typical Interruptions and Distractions

Interruptions and distractions can cause us to lose focus, become less productive, and make less progress toward our objectives. Typical disruptions and distractions include:

Email and Notifications: Constantly diverting our attention from crucial jobs and activities, email notifications, instant messages, and social media alerts can result in fragmented focus and lower productivity.

Multitasking: Trying to manage several things at once might cause cognitive overload and decreased productivity. We can't focus entirely on any one activity when multitasking, which leads to a decrease in productivity and a rise in mistakes.

Procrastination is the propensity to put off or postpone doing unpleasant, challenging, or daunting tasks. Procrastination frequently takes the form of putting off crucial work by participating in time-wasting or non-essential activities.

Unexpected Interruptions: We can lose our train of thought and interfere with our workflow when we receive unexpected calls, interruptions from coworkers, or interruptions from family members. These disruptions can vary in severity, from minor disruptions that need little care to more serious disruptions that take time and effort to resolve.

Environmental Factors: Uncomfortable surroundings, disarray, and noise can all interfere with our capacity to focus and pay attention. Maintaining focus and productivity can be difficult in a noisy or chaotic work environment.

We can design tactics and procedures to reduce common interruptions and distractions and improve the working environment by identifying them.

Methods for Reducing Distractions and Maintaining Attention

It takes discipline and the application of time- and attention-saving tactics to minimize distractions and maintain focus. The following strategies can help you reduce outside distractions and maintain focus:

Create a Distraction-Free Zone: Set off a specific area of your workspace where interruptions and distractions are avoided. Eliminate or reduce possible sources of distraction, such as noise, clutter, and technological devices, and establish a peaceful space that supports concentrated work.

Employ Time Blocking: Set aside certain time blocks for particular projects and activities, and make a commitment to concentrate only on those tasks during those times. Make use of methods like the Pomodoro Technique to work in concentrated bursts interspersed with regular pauses for rejuvenation.

Disable Notifications:

Turn off notifications that aren't absolutely necessary on your gadgets to reduce distractions and stay focused. Distractions such as social media alerts and email notifications should be turned off if they are going to take your focus away from crucial work.

Establish definite boundaries:

To guard against distractions and interruptions, clearly define boundaries for your time and attention. Let coworkers, friends, and family know when you are available, and set expectations for when you may be reached and when you need time to yourself.

Practice Mindfulness: To better handle distractions and maintain attention, cultivate mindfulness and awareness of your thoughts, emotions, and behaviors. Develop a focused, serene mindset that is less prone to distractions by engaging in practices like deep breathing, mindfulness, and meditation.

Task Prioritization: Sort tasks and activities according to their significance and urgency, and concentrate your time and energy on the most important tasks that support your aims and objectives. To distinguish between jobs that must be completed right away and those that may wait or be assigned, use strategies like the Eisenhower Matrix.

You can safeguard your time and attention, preserve productivity, and attain greater clarity and efficiency in your job and life by putting these strategies for reducing distractions and remaining focused into practice.

Delineating Limits and Establishing a Friendly Workplace

Minimizing distractions and interruptions and promoting focus and productivity require setting limits and establishing a favorable work environment. The following are some methods for establishing limits and fostering a positive work environment:

Establish Clearly Defined Work Hours: To distinguish between work and personal time, clearly define your work hours and boundaries. Tell coworkers, clients, and family members when you are available, and set expectations for when you can be contacted and when you need time to yourself.

Express Your Needs:

In the job, speak up for your demands and preferences by being upfront and aggressive in your communication with managers and coworkers. To encourage productivity and well-being, clearly communicate your limits, priorities, and preferences. Then, work with others to discover solutions that work for everyone.

Establish a Cozy Workspace:

Create a cozy, ergonomic workstation that encourages productivity, focus, and concentration. Make an investment in high-quality office supplies, lighting, and furniture, and decorate your workstation with objects that uplift and encourage you.

Reduce Distractions: Get rid of visual stimulation, noise, and clutter to reduce the amount of possible distractions in your workspace. Establish a peaceful, well-organized workstation that encourages focus and innovation. Get rid of or reduce distractions like electronics, pointless papers, and unrelated notifications.

Take Breaks and Rest: To avoid burnout and preserve productivity and wellbeing, give breaks and rest top priority. Plan regular pauses in your day to allow yourself to rest, recover, and revitalize. To help you relax and decompress, try deep breathing, stretches, and mindfulness exercises.

You may reduce interruptions and distractions, promote concentration and productivity, and establish a supportive environment for your priorities and goals by establishing boundaries and making your workspace accommodating.

Chapter 7

IMPROVING WORK-LIFE BALANCE

F*inding* a healthy balance between one's personal and professional lives is crucial to one's general fulfillment and well-being. The lines separating work and personal life can blur in today's fast-paced and connected world, which can cause stress, burnout, and discontent. It takes deliberate effort, self-awareness, and the use of methods and strategies to establish boundaries, create space, and give self-care and relaxation top priority in order to improve work-life balance. The significance of work-life balance for general well-being, methods for establishing boundaries and separating work from personal life, and methods for introducing self-care and relaxation into your daily routine are all covered in this chapter.

Work-Life Balance Is Essential for General Well-Being

The equilibrium between the demands of work and personal life—including family, relationships, interests, and leisure activities—is referred to as work-life balance. Achieving a healthy work-life balance is crucial for happiness and general well-being because it enables people to fulfill their obligations without compromising their mental, emotional, or physical health. It also enables them to follow their hobbies and maintain their relationships. The following justifies the significance of work-life balance for general wellbeing:

Decreased Stress and Burnout: Reducing stress and preventing burnout can be achieved by keeping a healthy balance between work and personal life. Prolonged stress brought on by obligations at work can have a detrimental effect on one's quality of life, mental and physical well-being. People can lessen their risk of burnout and tiredness by setting limits and giving priority to their personal time and hobbies.

Better Physical Health: Work-life balance has been linked to improved physical health outcomes, including a lower risk of chronic illnesses including diabetes, obesity, and heart disease. Exercise, relaxation techniques, and leisure pursuits all contribute to physical well-being and improve general health and energy.

Improved Mental Health: Maintaining a work-life balance leads to improved mental health outcomes, such as a decrease in the signs and symptoms of anxiety, depression, and mood disorders. Taking pauses, spending time with close friends and family, and engaging in interests and hobbies offer chances for emotional fulfillment, enjoyment, and relaxation—all of which support resilience and mental health.

Increased Satisfaction and Fulfillment: Living a balanced personal and professional life results in increased levels of fulfillment and satisfaction in all facets of life. People are happier and have a more complete existence when they feel appreciated, supported, and content both at work and at home.

Greater Relationships: By enabling people to prioritize meaningful connections and quality time, work-life balance helps people build greater relationships with their loved ones, family, and friends. Interpersonal connections are strengthened and enhanced through spending time together, exchanging experiences, and engaging in common activities.

Enhanced Creativity and Productivity: Keeping a work-life balance improves performance in both personal and professional endeavors. It also increases creativity and productivity. Taking pauses, having fun, and pursuing hobbies improve cognitive function, increase energy, and foster creativity, which increases productivity and effectiveness at work and in life.

In general, a work-life balance allows people to enjoy happy, purposeful, and meaningful lives, which is crucial for their general well-being.

Techniques for Determining Limits and Keeping Work and Personal Life Apart

Maintaining work-life balance and preventing job-related stressors from intruding into personal time requires setting boundaries and establishing a clear division between work and personal life. The following are some methods for establishing limits and fostering distance:

Establish Clearly Defined Work Hours: To distinguish between work and personal time, clearly define your work hours and boundaries. Let coworkers, clients, and superiors know when you are available, and set expectations for when you can be reached and when you need time to yourself.

Establish a Dedicated Workspace: To establish a mental and physical barrier between work and personal life, set aside a specific area for work-related tasks. Select a peaceful, comfortable space that is free from interruptions and noise, and dedicate that space only to work-related activities.

Minimize Communications About Work:
To reduce the amount of job-related stress that intrudes into personal time, limit communications connected to work that take place outside of scheduled work hours. Disable email notifications, establish guidelines for answering work-related messages, and let coworkers and managers know your availability and preferences.

Practice Transitional Rituals: Create transitional rituals to indicate the conclusion of the workday and the start of personal time. Create routines that help you psychologically and emotionally shift from work mode to relaxation mode. Some examples of these rituals include turning off your computer, changing out of your work attire, or taking a stroll.

Arrange Personal Time and Activities: Make personal time and activities a top priority by putting them on your calendar and considering them as unchangeable obligations. To make sure you have time to relax and rejuvenate away from work, schedule time for hobbies, pastimes, and self-care routines.

Establish Digital limits: Establish digital limits to reduce the amount of time that technology and digital gadgets take up during personal time. Create tech-free zones in your home and set rules around device use, such as turning off electronics during meals, family time, and leisure activities.

By putting these boundary-setting and division techniques into practice, you may safeguard your time, energy, and well-being while also attaining a better feeling of fulfillment and balance in both spheres of your life.

Including Relaxation and Self-Care in Your Daily Routine

Reducing stress, fostering general well-being, and preserving work-life balance all depend on you making time for self-care and relaxation. While relaxation techniques aid in fostering a state of quiet and tranquility and lessen the negative effects of stress on the body and mind, self-care refers to practices and activities that support one's emotional, mental, and physical well-being. Here are some methods to add relaxation and self-care to your daily routine:

Make Sleep a Priority: Make sleep a priority by setting up a regular sleep routine and furnishing a comfortable sleeping space. Try to get seven to nine hours of good sleep every night. To help you do this, try deep breathing exercises, progressive muscular relaxation, or meditation.

Exercise: Regular exercise will improve your physical health, lower your stress level, and give you more energy and happiness. Include physical activities like cycling, yoga, jogging, or walking in your daily routine. Make exercise and movement a priority as part of your self-care routine.

Practice Mindfulness and Meditation: To develop awareness, lower stress levels, and encourage focus and mental clarity, practice mindfulness and meditation. Make time each day for mindfulness meditation or guided relaxation activities. To help you relax and calm down, try deep breathing, body scanning, or visualization.

Nurture connections: Spend quality time with loved ones, have deep talks, and partake in activities as a way to nurture your connections with them. As part of your self-care regimen, prioritize relationships and social support, and look for community-building and connection-building possibilities.

Enjoy Your Interests and Hobbies: Schedule time for the things that make you happy and fulfilled, such as creative endeavors, interests, and hobbies. Painting, gardening, music-making, cooking—all of these things are soul-nourishing and give you a sense of purpose and accomplishment—should be your top priorities.

Practice Gratitude and Self-Compassion: As part of your self-care regimen, acknowledge your blessings, successes, and strengths. You should also work on maintaining a positive view on life. Every day, set aside some time to think about your blessings and to show yourself and other people compassion and kindness.

You may lower stress, increase wellbeing, and improve your general quality of life by making self-care and relaxation a part of your daily routine. Prioritize self-care and make a commitment to promoting your mental, emotional, and physical well-being as part of your continuous pursuit of fulfillment and a work-life balance.

Chapter 8

TRACKING PROGRESS AND ADJUSTING STRATEGIES

P*roductivity* and efficient time management depend on monitoring results and modifying tactics. You may maximize your productivity, effectiveness, and general success by keeping an eye on and assessing your work, making modifications in response to input and outcomes, and iteratively improving your time management strategy. This chapter covers the significance of monitoring progress and making necessary adjustments to strategies, as well as methods for keeping an eye on and assessing your productivity and time management efforts. It also covers how to make adjustments based on feedback and outcomes and continuously improve your time management system for maximum efficacy.

Tracking and Assessing Your Productivity and Time Management Efforts

It's essential to track and assess your productivity and time management endeavors in order to pinpoint your advantages, disadvantages, and potential growth areas. You can obtain insights into your routines, behaviors, and productivity levels by monitoring important indicators, evaluating your progress, and seeing patterns and trends. The following methods can be used to track and assess your productivity and time management efforts:

Maintain a Time journal: To keep track of your daily activities, maintain a thorough time journal. Keep track of the things you do, how long you spend on them, and any interruptions or diversions that happen. Examine your time log on a regular basis to spot trends, inefficiencies, and areas that could use improvement.

Employ Tools for Productivity:
To monitor your progress and gauge your productivity, make use of productivity tools and apps. To keep an eye on your work, check your progress, and evaluate your productivity over time, use tools like time tracking applications, task management software, and project management platforms.

Establish and Evaluate Objectives:
Establish measurable, well-defined objectives for your time management and productivity endeavors, and periodically assess your advancement towards these targets. Evaluate your progress toward your goals, note any roadblocks or difficulties, and modify your approach as necessary to keep on course.

Conduct Regular evaluations: To evaluate the efficacy of your time management and productivity techniques and pinpoint areas for development, conduct regular evaluations. Evaluate your current situation and identify areas for improvement, get input from mentors or coworkers, and apply the lessons you've learnt to your next endeavors.

Analyze Performance indicators: To assess your efficacy and productivity, examine performance indicators including turnaround times, completion rates, and work quality. Examine your performance data for trends and patterns. Then, utilize this knowledge to pinpoint problem areas and create enhancement plans.

You may obtain important insights into your habits, behaviors, and performance by tracking and analyzing your time management and productivity efforts. This can help you find areas for development and make well-informed decisions about how to maximize your effectiveness and efficiency.

Modifying in Response to Input and Outcomes

It is imperative to make modifications in response to input and outcomes in order to adjust to evolving situations, tackle obstacles, and enhance your time management and productivity techniques. You may improve your efficacy and enhance your strategies by getting input from others, examining your performance statistics, and being willing to try new things. The following methods can be used to modify based on input and outcomes:

Request Feedback: Ask mentors, bosses, or coworkers for their opinions on your time-management and productivity strategies. Seek particular advice or recommendations for enhancement, and be receptive to proposals for development and constructive criticism.

Evaluate Your Performance: To pinpoint areas in need of development and growth prospects, evaluate your performance and outcomes on a regular basis. Think about what is good and what could be better, then come up with some possible improvement tactics.

Try Out Novel Strategies:

Try out some new methods, strategies, or resources to enhance your productivity and time management. Be open to experimenting with various approaches, plans, or frameworks, and assess their efficacy in light of feedback and outcomes.

Analyze Performance Data: To find trends, patterns, and areas for improvement, analyze performance data such as completion rates, turnaround times, and work quality. Make decisions based on this data, giving priority to changes that will affect your effectiveness and productivity the most.

Iterate and Iterate: Adjust your productivity and time management strategies frequently in response to criticism and outcomes. To maximize your productivity and efficacy over time, keep improving your tactics, trying out novel ideas, and adjusting to new situations.

You may enhance your time management and productivity techniques, respond to obstacles, and adjust to changing situations by basing your decisions on feedback and outcomes. This will help you succeed and feel more fulfilled in both your personal and professional lives.

Iteratively Improving Your Time Management Framework for Maximum Efficiency

To keep your time management system operating at its best throughout time, you must constantly improve it. Your time management requirements may change as your priorities, obligations, and circumstances do, necessitating modifications to your tactics and techniques. Maintaining adaptability, flexibility, and an open mind will help you create a time management strategy that suits your particular requirements and preferences. The following strategies will help you make constant improvements to your time management strategy for maximum efficacy:

Evaluate Your Needs: To make sure that your time management system is in line with your goals and present situation, evaluate your needs, priorities, and goals on a regular basis. Take into account variables like modifications in workload, due dates, or personal obligations, and modify your tactics correspondingly.

Get Input: Consult with coworkers, mentors, or reliable advisors to get their opinions on your time management procedures and framework. Seek advice or recommendations for enhancement, and remain open to criticism that can help you hone your tactics.

Try New Tools: To improve the efficacy of your time management, try out new tools, methods, or systems. Keep up with advancements in time management techniques and technology, and be open to experimenting with new strategies that could boost your output and efficiency.

Consider the Lessons Acquired:

Think back on the things you've learnt from the past and modify your time management strategies accordingly. Take into account what has previously worked effectively and what may be improved, then apply these realizations to your continuous attempts to enhance your time management system.

Remain Adaptive and Flexible: as it comes to managing your time, remain adaptable and flexible. You should be prepared to modify your plans as necessary to take into account new priorities or situations. Adopt a growth attitude that sees obstacles as chances for development and learning, and be willing to try out novel strategies to maximize your efficiency.
Through constant improvement of your time management system, you may overcome obstacles, adjust to changing conditions, and increase productivity and efficiency in both your personal and professional life.

Chapter 9

EMPOWERING YOUR TIME MANAGEMENT JOURNEY

I'm glad you finished "Time Management and Productivity: Mastering Your Time for Maximum Efficiency." You've started a life-changing adventure to maximize your productivity, take back control of your schedule, and find more fulfillment and balance. Let's review the main ideas and techniques discussed in this ebook as we draw to a close, consider how important it is to act on what you've learned, and offer resources for more reading and assistance to help you on your ongoing time management journey.

Summary of the Main Ideas and Techniques the Ebook Covers

We've covered a wide range of ideas, methods, and approaches in this booklet to help you become an expert time manager and increase your productivity. Below is a summary of some of the main ideas and techniques discussed:

Comprehending Time Management: We delved into the meaning and importance of time management, highlighting its role in accomplishing individual and professional objectives, decreasing anxiety, and improving general health.

Techniques for Prioritization, Goal-Setting, To-Do Lists, and Time Blocking are some of the Strategies for Effective Time Management that we covered in order to help you manage your time and resources more effectively.

Increasing Productivity: In order to increase productivity and get better attention and efficiency in both your work and life, we looked at strategies for fighting procrastination, controlling energy levels, and utilizing technology.

Time Blocking and Scheduling: We looked at the fundamentals and advantages of time blocking, talked about how to make daily and weekly calendars for optimal productivity, and looked at how flexible and adaptive scheduling can be to handle unforeseen changes.

Managing Distractions and Interruptions: We talked about typical sources of distractions and interruptions and offered tips on how to reduce them, maintain focus, and set up a productive workspace.

Enhancing Work-Life Balance: In order to attain more harmony and fulfillment, we underlined the significance of work-life balance for general well-being and offered techniques for establishing boundaries, separating work and personal life, and incorporating self-care and relaxation into your daily routine.

Tracking Progress and Modifying Strategies: We looked at how important it is to keep an eye on and assess your time management efforts, alter your plan in response to criticism and outcomes, and keep improving it until it works as best it can.

Motivation to Act and Put What Has Been Learned Into Practice

It's time to put what you've learned into practice and apply time management tactics and principles to your everyday life now that you have a thorough understanding of them. Recall that information is just potential if it is not used. Here are some words of inspiration to motivate you to move forward:

Start Small: Choose one or two core tactics that you find compelling and make a commitment to incorporate them into your everyday practice. Whether it's time blocking, SMART goal planning, or reducing distractions, little adjustments over time can have a big impact.

Remain Steady:
The secret to effective time management is consistency. Despite obstacles or disappointments, resolve to regularly use the methods and approaches you've learnt. Keep in mind that advancement is the result of consistent, gradual work over time.

Being an expert in time management takes effort and persistence, just like Rome wasn't built in a day. As you progress through the highs and lows of your time management journey, be kind to yourself and don't give up on your ambitions to get better.

Honor Your Advancement:
No matter how minor they may seem, acknowledge and celebrate your accomplishments and milestones along the path. Acknowledge your accomplishments and the constructive adjustments you've made, then draw inspiration from them to keep aiming for even more effectiveness and efficiency.

You may become an expert at managing your time and reach optimum efficiency in all facets of your life by acting on what you've learned.

Additional Reading and Supporting Resources

You might find it beneficial to look into further resources and assistance as you proceed on your time management journey in order to improve your knowledge and abilities. The following resources can be used for additional reading or help:

Books: James Clear's "Atomic Habits"
"Deep Work: Rules for Focused Success in a Distracted World" written by Cal Newport
Stephen R. Covey's "The 7 Habits of Highly Effective People"
"**Getting Things Done:** The Art of Stress-Free Productivity" written by David Allen
Online Courses: LinkedIn's Time Management Fundamentals Acquiring Productivity Getting Things Done (GTD) Masterclass on Udemy Course on Coursera Applications and Tools:
Todoist: Project and Task Coordinator
Toggl: Reporting and Time Monitoring
Woods: Remain Alert and Present
Support and Community:
Participate in online groups or forums devoted to productivity and time management to meet like-minded people, trade advice, and share experiences.
To assist you reach your objectives, think about getting support from a time management coach or mentor who can offer direction, responsibility, and customized techniques.
Recall that there's always space for development and progress on the never-ending path to time management mastery. Continue to be inquisitive, dedicated, and to aim for perfection in whatever you do.

Finally

As we come to an end of our investigation into productivity and time management, I would like to thank you for your hard work and devotion to making the most of your time and reaching your highest level of efficiency. You've made a proactive move in the direction of more success, fulfillment, and balance in both your personal and professional life by putting the methods and tactics in this booklet into practice.

Recall that time is our most valuable resource, and our life's quality is ultimately determined by the way we choose to use it. In addition to increasing your output and effectiveness, time management allows you to make time for your hobbies, take care of your relationships, and live a purposeful life.

I urge you to adopt the ideas and methods presented in this booklet and to keep learning, trying, and improving how you handle productivity and time management. You have the ability to change the way you relate to time and build a happy, fulfilling life with a commitment to lifelong learning, effort, and dedication.

I appreciate you coming along on this adventure with me, and I wish you all the success and joy in the world as you keep learning how to manage your time well and work as efficiently as possible. Cheers to an infinite future full of opportunities and promise.

---

www.ingramcontent.com/pod-product-compliance
Lightning Source LLC
Chambersburg PA
CBHW062207220526
45470CB00009B/2955